Welcome to Year 6 cursive handwriting. Here you'll find lots of tips on how to make your writing faster and more legible.

You'll also get to explore some of the wonders of the world! Fill in your passport first.

Name: ______________________________

Address: ______________________________

____

____

Date of birth: ______________________________

Nationality: ______________________________

Height: ______________________________

Eye colour: ______________________________

Distinguishing characteristics: ______________________________

____

____

____

Current photograph:

Progressive speed trials

Copy this text into the lines below. Have a classmate time you. Then assess the fluency and legibility of your writing.

Date __ /__ /__ Time taken: ___ seconds

The world contains amazing things – landforms and structures that have to be seen to be believed!

Rate your fluency. Rate your legibility.

Date __ /__ /__ Time taken: ___ seconds

The world contains amazing things – landforms and structures that have to be seen to be believed!

Rate your fluency. Rate your legibility.

Date __ /__ /__ Time taken: ___ seconds

The world contains amazing things – landforms and structures that have to be seen to be believed!

Rate your fluency. Rate your legibility.

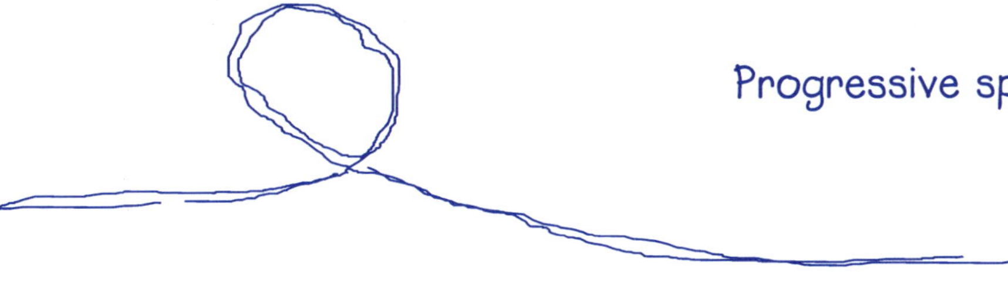

Date __ /__ /__ Time taken: ___ seconds

The world contains amazing things — landforms and structures that have to be seen to be believed!

Rate your fluency.

Rate your legibility.

Date __ /__ /__ Time taken: ___ seconds

The world contains amazing things — landforms and structures that have to be seen to be believed!

Rate your fluency.

Rate your legibility.

Date __ /__ /__ Time taken: ___ seconds

The world contains amazing things — landforms and structures that have to be seen to be believed!

Rate your fluency.

Rate your legibility.

Revision – Letter formation

Date ___ / ___ / ___

Using 8 mm lines is easy if you remember to divide the space above the line into thirds. The letter bodies sit in the bottom section, and the letter heads sit in the middle section.

The top section allows space for the tails of letters from the line above!

A a B b C c D d E e F f G g

H h I i J j K k L l M m N n

O o P p Q q R r S s T t U u

V v W w X x Y y Z z

Get ready to explore the wonders of the world!

1 2 3 4 5 6 7 8 9 10 20 30 40 50 60 70 80 90 100

SELF ASSESSMENT Rate your printing.

☆ Needs work

☆☆ Monumental effort

☆☆☆ Spectacular!

Date ___ / ___ / ___

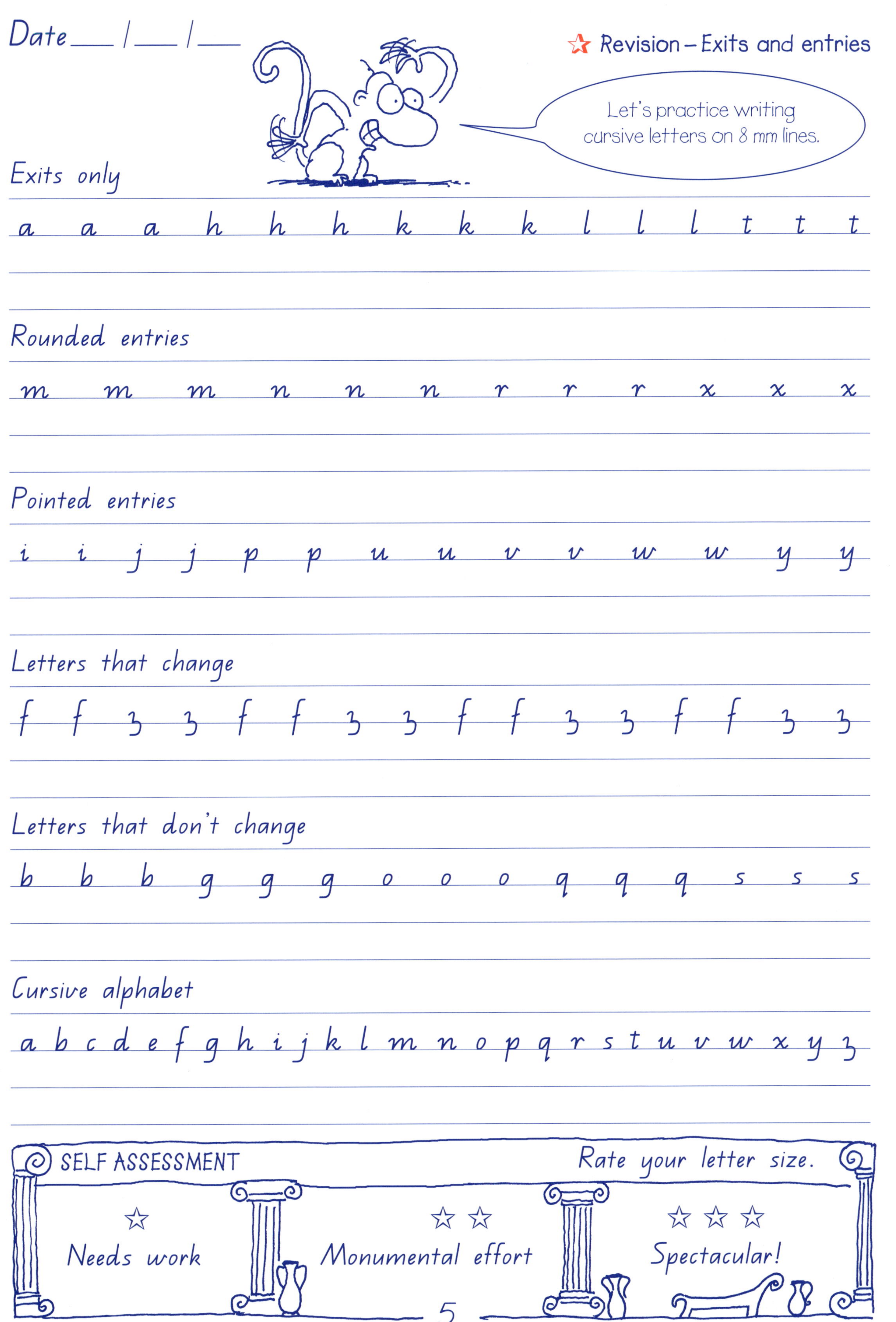

Exits only

a a a h h h k k k l l l t t t

Rounded entries

m m m n n n r r r x x x

Pointed entries

i i j j p p u u v v w w y y

Letters that change

f f z z f f z z f f z z f f z z

Letters that don't change

b b b g g g o o o q q q s s s

Cursive alphabet

a b c d e f g h i j k l m n o p q r s t u v w x y z

SELF ASSESSMENT

Rate your letter size.

☆ Needs work

☆☆ Monumental effort

☆☆☆ Spectacular!

Date ___ / ___ / ___

45°

an

45°

am in ur cr ex kn mm dr em ux

ax en ir mn ar ix um er un im

ram tan into number knot crimson

ember limb fit immense stick mnemonic

Many people travel far and wide to see the wondrous

and incredible sights that are found throughout the

world.

SELF ASSESSMENT

Circle your best diagonal join.

Date ___ / ___ / ___

ti hu ai ip cy du aw ki mi ly

ap ci my ew hi up ty av ky ni

tiny knitter dump tuner deep shiver hive

The world contains many wonderful things. The Wonders of the World include Earth's spectacular natural features (like Uluru), plus amazing structures built by people (like the Great Wall of China).

Date ___ / ___ / ___

When you do a diagonal join to a head and body letter, go right to the top of the letter, then retrace a bit on your way back down.

TICKETS

el (retrace) nk (retrace)

th it ck nk ab nt tl et ht lt

title element mink untimely little minty

think clunky leek likely climb imminent

The Great Pyramid at Giza is the only one of the Seven Wonders of the Ancient World that is still standing today.

SELF ASSESSMENT

Circle your best diagonal join to a head and body letter.

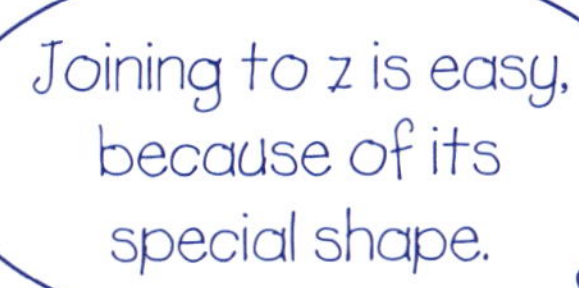

Remember that z has a rounded entry and a tail like g, j and y.

haze

az ez iz uz az ez iz uz az iz

maze razor doze size czar prize sneeze

hazy seize graze hazel froze crazy brazen

hazard breeze dozen azure azalea amazing

buzzard dizzy fuzzy pizza jazz pizzazz

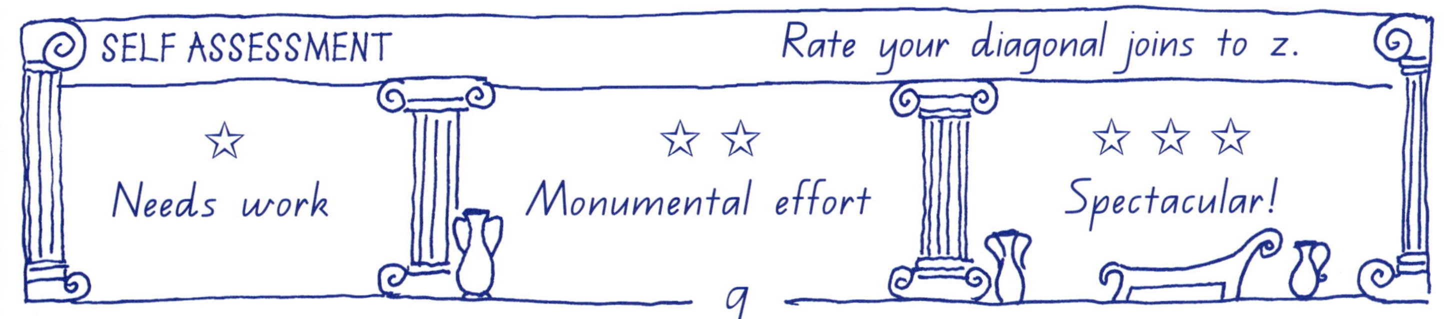

Date ___ / ___ / ___

When you join diagonally to s, remember to modify the s by making the top shorter.

is ks

ns es ts is as ks ds ls ms us

trains tunes history lasting tracks feeds

poles terms bustle lanes resting beans

villains tonsils claims sausages distances

figures artist circles places was landscape

The Mausoleum at Halicarnassus – the huge tomb of governor Mausolus – was made mainly of marble.

SELF ASSESSMENT

Underline the word that contains your best diagonal join to modified s.

Date ___ / ___ / ___

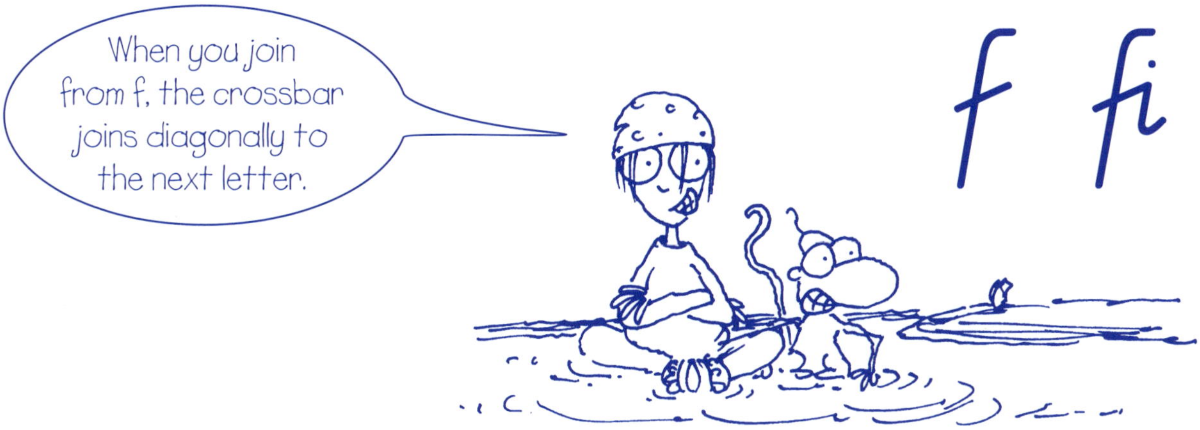
When you join from f, the crossbar joins diagonally to the next letter.

f fi fe

fe fi fo fu fl fr ft fe fi fo

furry fiend feeble flea friendly flautist

The Dead Sea is so salty, fish can't survive in it. The saltiness makes the water very buoyant, so it's fun to float in. You'll find you can sit in it as though you're sitting in a bean bag.

SELF ASSESSMENT
Rate your joins from f.
☆ Needs work
☆☆ Monumental effort
☆☆☆ Spectacular!

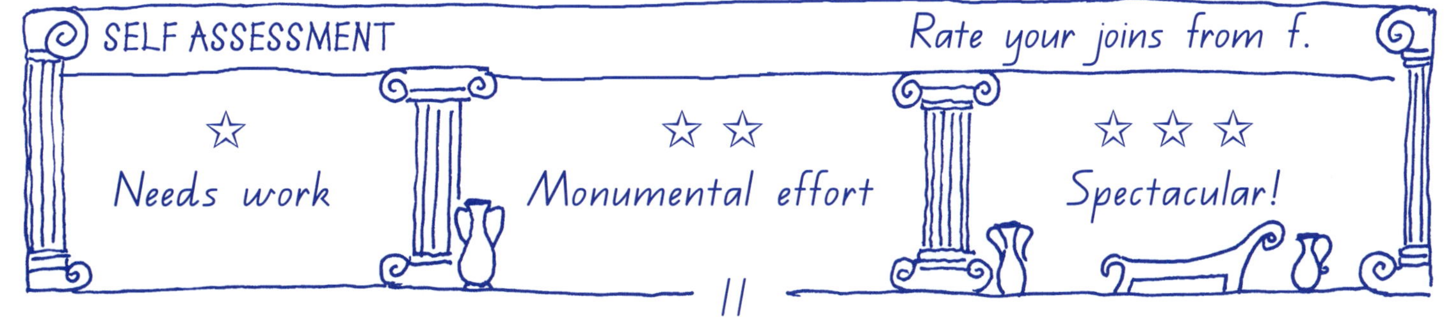

☆ Revision – Diagonal joins to modified f

Date ___ / ___ / ___

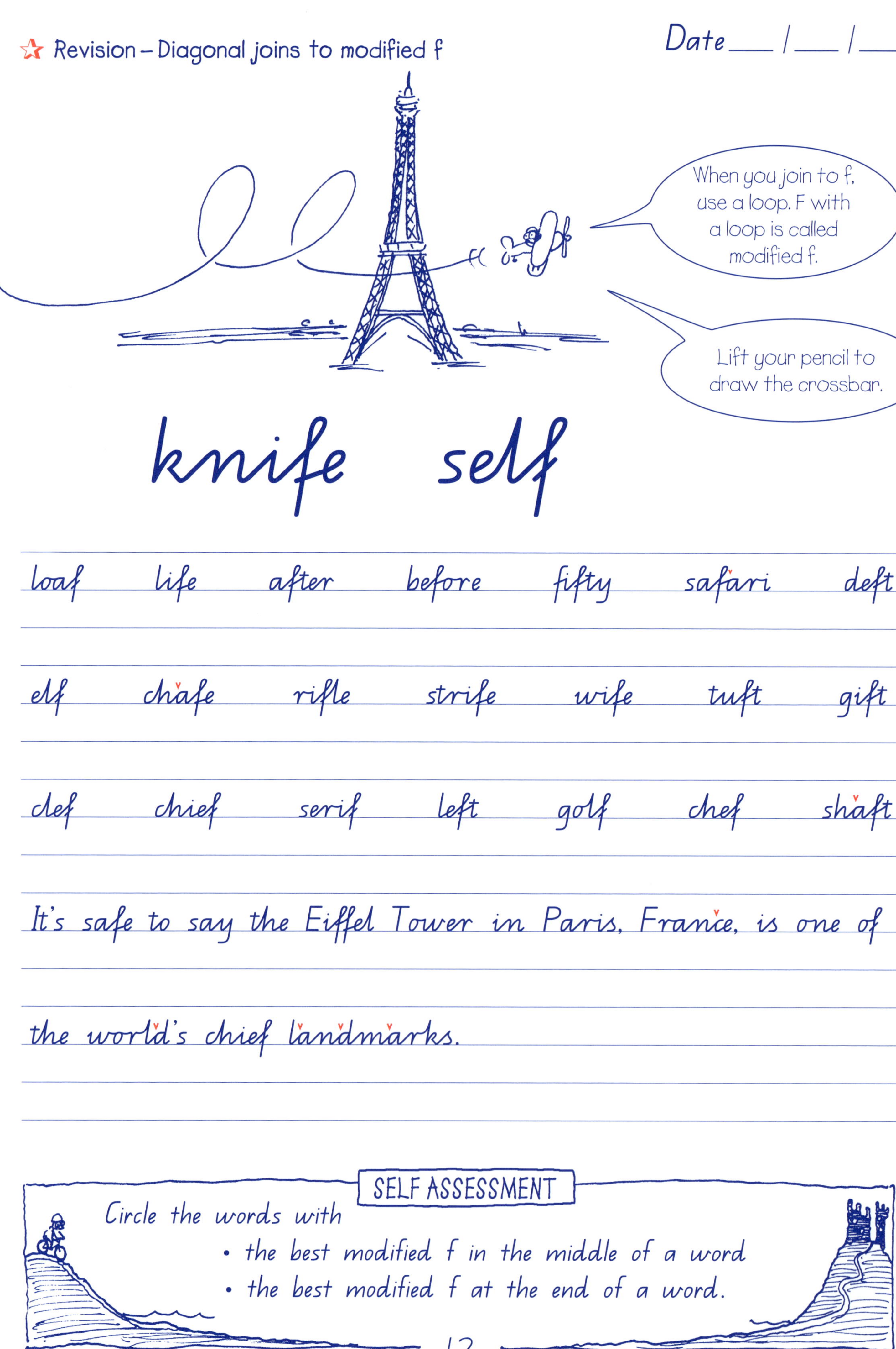

knife self

loaf life after before fifty safari deft

elf chafe rifle strife wife tuft gift

clef chief serif left golf chef shaft

It's safe to say the Eiffel Tower in Paris, France, is one of the world's chief landmarks.

SELF ASSESSMENT

Circle the words with

- the best modified f in the middle of a word
- the best modified f at the end of a word.

Date ___ / ___ / ___

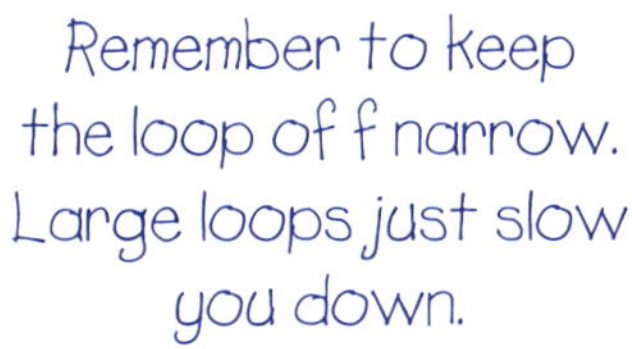

office ruffle

aff eff iff off uff aff eff iff off

sniff buff diff baffle daffodil traffic

stuffing raffish truffle effort puffy muffler

The Pharos at Alexandria was a terrifically tall lighthouse that burned wood to afford light. It was very effective – the light could be seen 55km off.

Date ___ / ___ / ___

The letters a, c, d, g, and q are dropped onto a letter with an exit.

ma ic

ed ng eq ca ka nd ac dg ic ha

sing need cattle under click hedge clear

aqua nudge danger half tangy nothing

The Hanging Gardens of Babylon were said to have been built by King Nebuchadnezzar II for his wife, Amytis, to remind her of home.

SELF ASSESSMENT

Circle your best drop-on join.

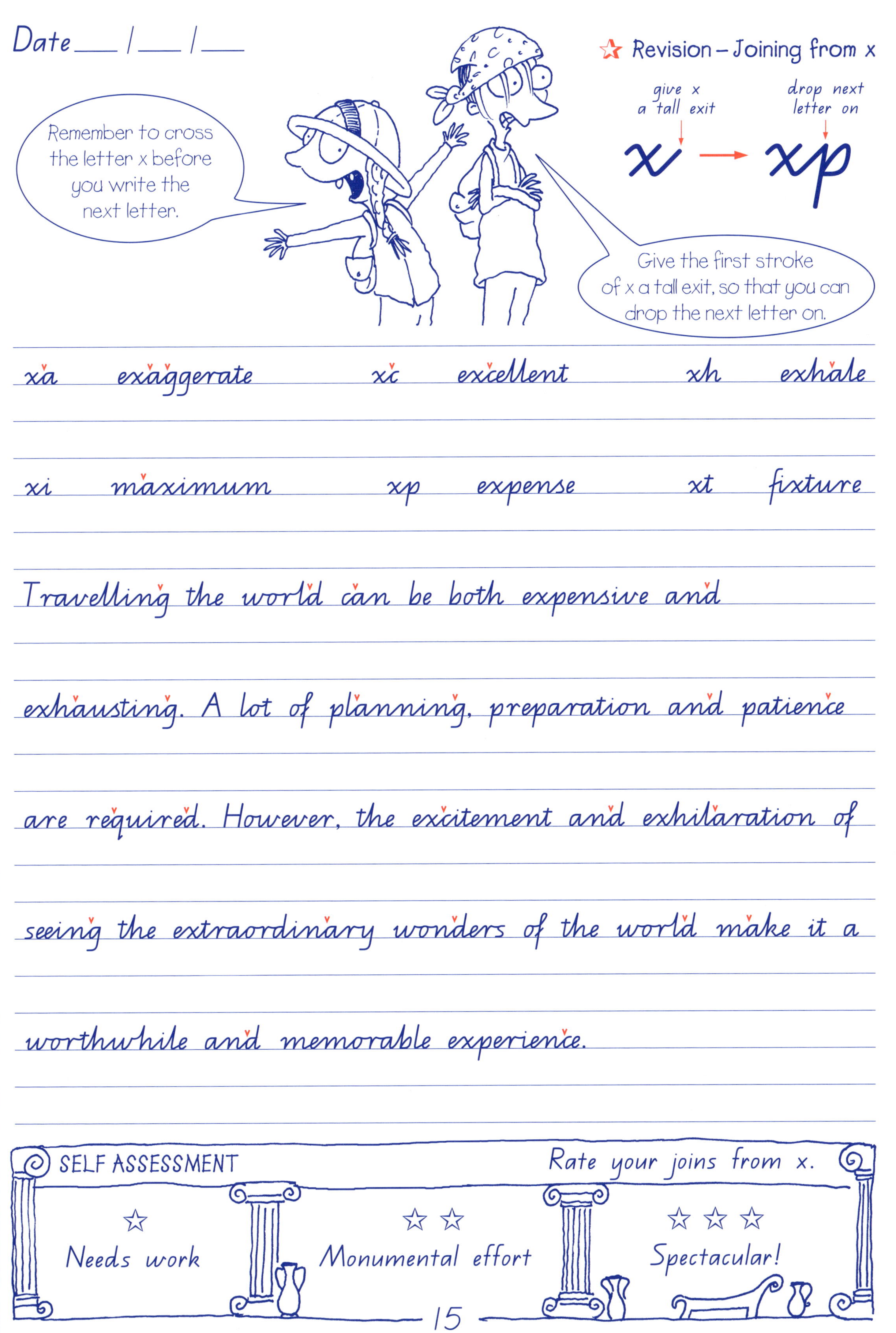

Date ___ / ___ / ___
Revision – Joining from x
give x a tall exit
drop next letter on
x → xp
Remember to cross the letter x before you write the next letter.
Give the first stroke of x a tall exit, so that you can drop the next letter on.
xa exaggerate xc excellent xh exhale
xi maximum xp expense xt fixture
Travelling the world can be both expensive and
exhausting. A lot of planning, preparation and patience
are required. However, the excitement and exhilaration of
seeing the extraordinary wonders of the world make it a
worthwhile and memorable experience.
SELF ASSESSMENT
Rate your joins from x.
☆ Needs work
☆☆ Monumental effort
☆☆☆ Spectacular!

Date ___ / ___ / ___

small dip

rn vi

on rn vi wn op ru wr rm ou wi

vital monkey yawning toxin mouse ooze

wiry armour onion vicious furry worm

The statue of Zeus at Olympia contained over a tonne of gold. It also contained ivory from elephants' tusks and hippopotamuses' teeth.

SELF ASSESSMENT

Underline your three best horizontal joins.

Date ___ /___ /___

ro oc va oa rd wa rg ra wo od

knock moat urgent radar waxy vampire

prodded arch waist ogre value crate

The statue of Zeus, king of the Greek gods, was worth a fortune. It was also enormous, at 13m high – taller than a four-storey house!

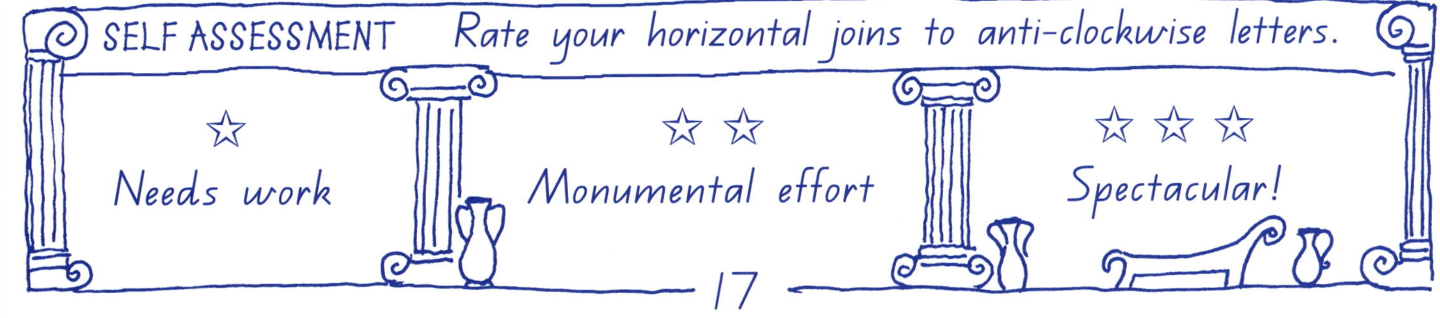

Date ___ / ___ / ___

ws rs os ws rs os ws rs os

bowser shivers poster claws torso solos

years engineers orders nostril frosty rows

For years, travellers to southern England have admired

the huge White Horse that is carved into the chalk

hillside above the town of Uffington.

SELF ASSESSMENT

Circle the word with the best horizontal join to s.

Date ___ / ___ / ___

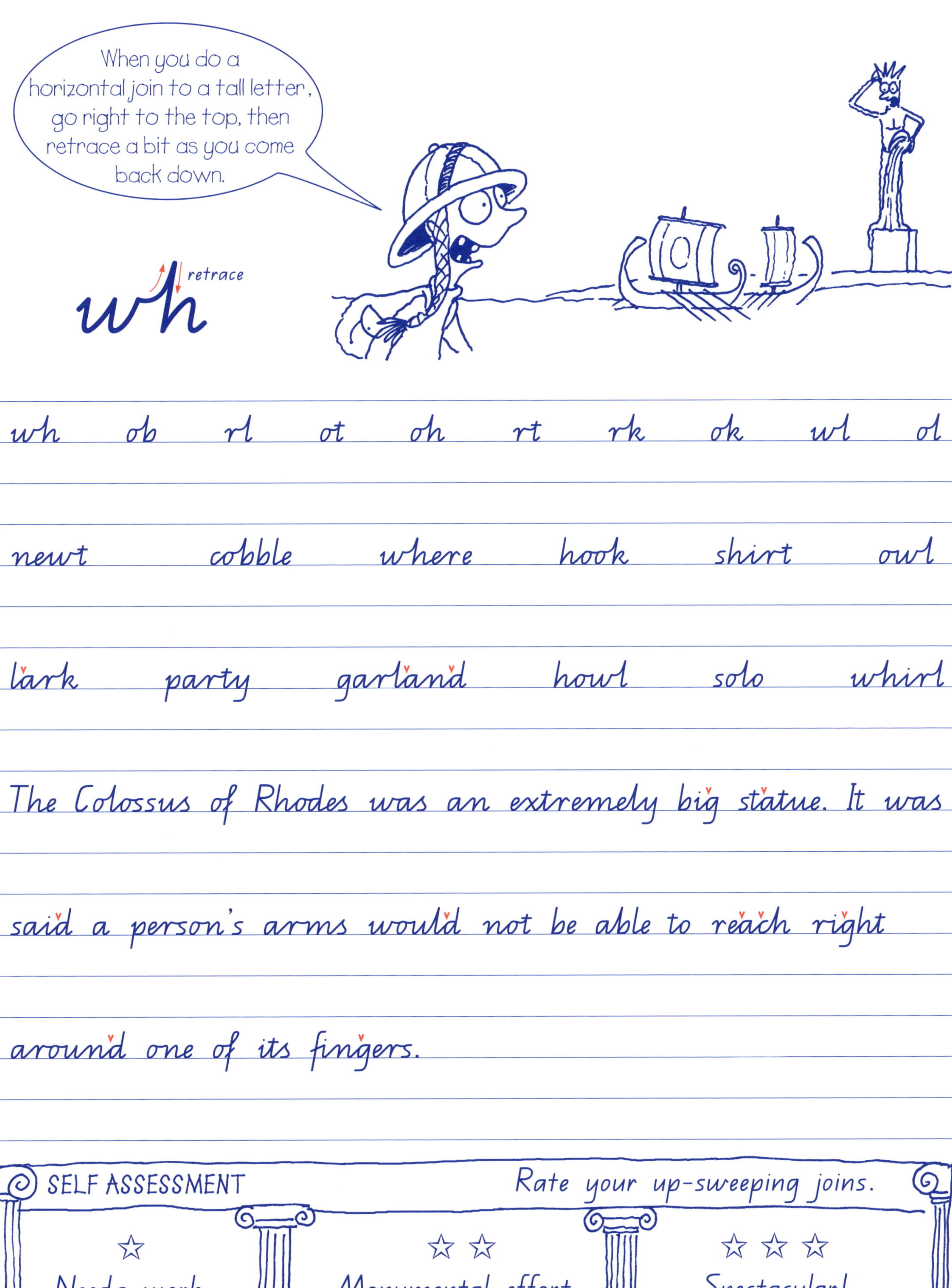

wh ob rl ot oh rt rk ok wl ol

newt cobble where hook shirt owl

lark party garland howl solo whirl

The Colossus of Rhodes was an extremely big statue. It was

said a person's arms would not be able to reach right

around one of its fingers.

SELF ASSESSMENT

Rate your up-sweeping joins.

☆	☆ ☆	☆ ☆ ☆
Needs work	Monumental effort	Spectacular!

☆ Revision – Letters that don't join

Date ___ / ___ / ___

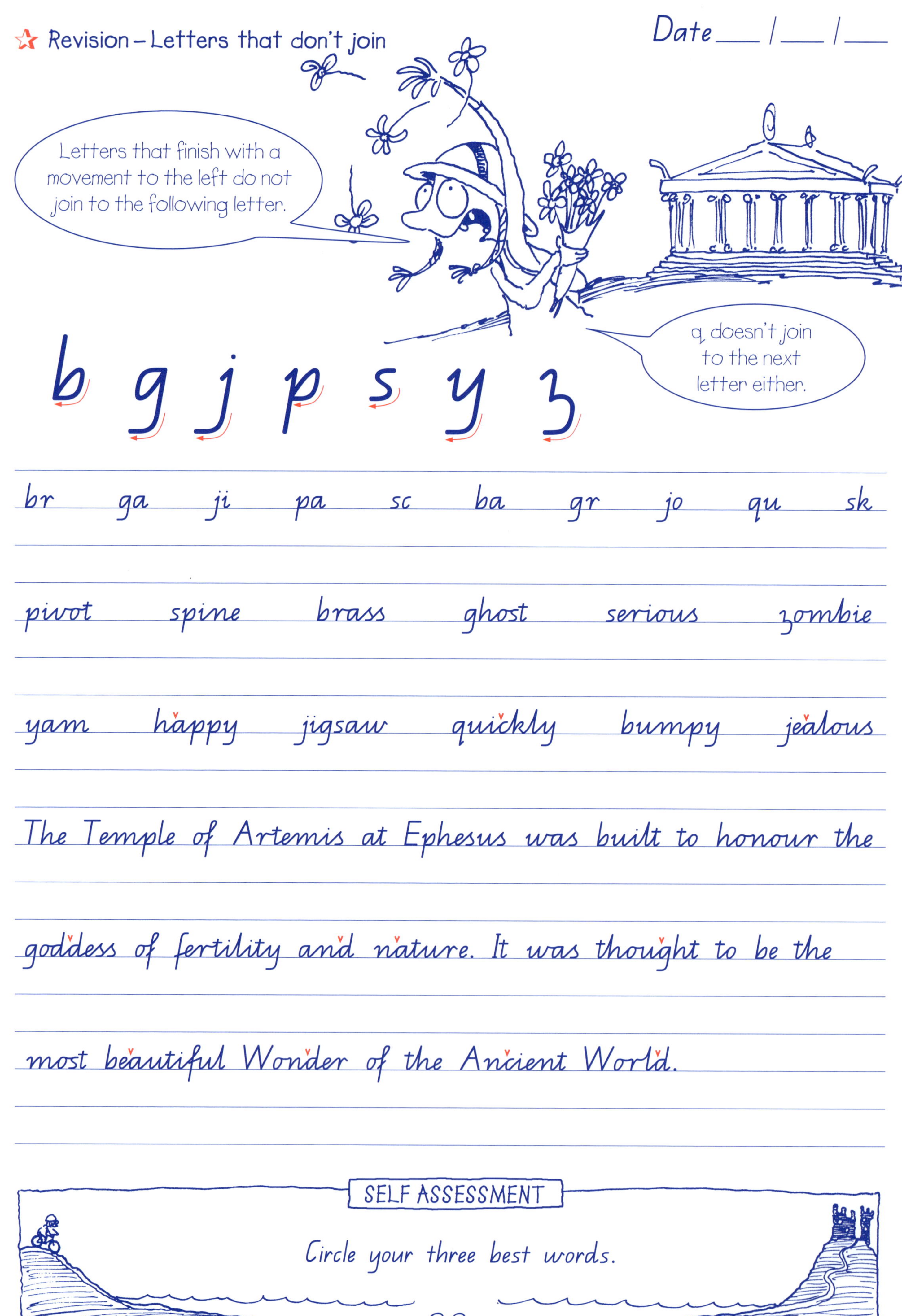

b g j p s y z

br ga ji pa sc ba gr jo qu sk

pivot spine brass ghost serious zombie

yam happy jigsaw quickly bumpy jealous

The Temple of Artemis at Ephesus was built to honour the goddess of fertility and nature. It was thought to be the most beautiful Wonder of the Ancient World.

SELF ASSESSMENT

Circle your three best words.

Date ___ / ___ / ___

re we

oe re ve we oe re ve we oe re

recent mangoes green cavern tower overt

regal welcome verve revel weasel reflexes

There are very many secret chambers within the Great Pyramid at Giza. The King's body and treasure were stolen from one chamber by robbers.

Assessment page – Joins

Date ___ / ___ / ___

Write each word in cursive.

Diagonal joins

funky lemur unlikely destiny clump muzzle

Drop-on joins

under mince candle magnify aquatic delicacy

Horizontal joins

woman moon horizon whom flavour bowl

Top-finishers don't join to e

weekly event ferret mixer twenty awesome dominoes

Joining to s

terse crispy monsters flashy browse ostriches

Joining to and from f

find furtive left fruitful ruffle waffle

Letters that don't join

purple scab blister jelly grabs quick zest

Teacher

Date ___ / ___ / ___

Speed test 

Read the sentence below, and memorise it if you can. Write out the sentence as many times as you can in 2 minutes. Have a classmate time you.

There were many other wonders in the Ancient World besides those included in the familiar list of seven.

Total number of words: ________

Divide by two for speed in words per minute: ________

SELF ASSESSMENT

Rate your fluency.

☆ ☆☆ ☆☆☆

Rate your legibility.

☆ ☆☆ ☆☆☆

Date ___ / ___ / ___

Look at the words below. Circle the words that have an even letter size.

slink towel reach brisk smash gargle bulb

Did you find words with an even letter size easier to read?

☐ Yes ☐ No

Copy. Remember to keep your letters an even size.

cheat elbow thank fumble absorb yellow

One of the wonders of the modern world is the Channel

Tunnel that links Great Britain and France. The main

tunnels lie about 45m beneath the seabed of the English

Channel.

SELF ASSESSMENT

Tick the line that has the most consistent letter size.

Date ___ / ___ / ___

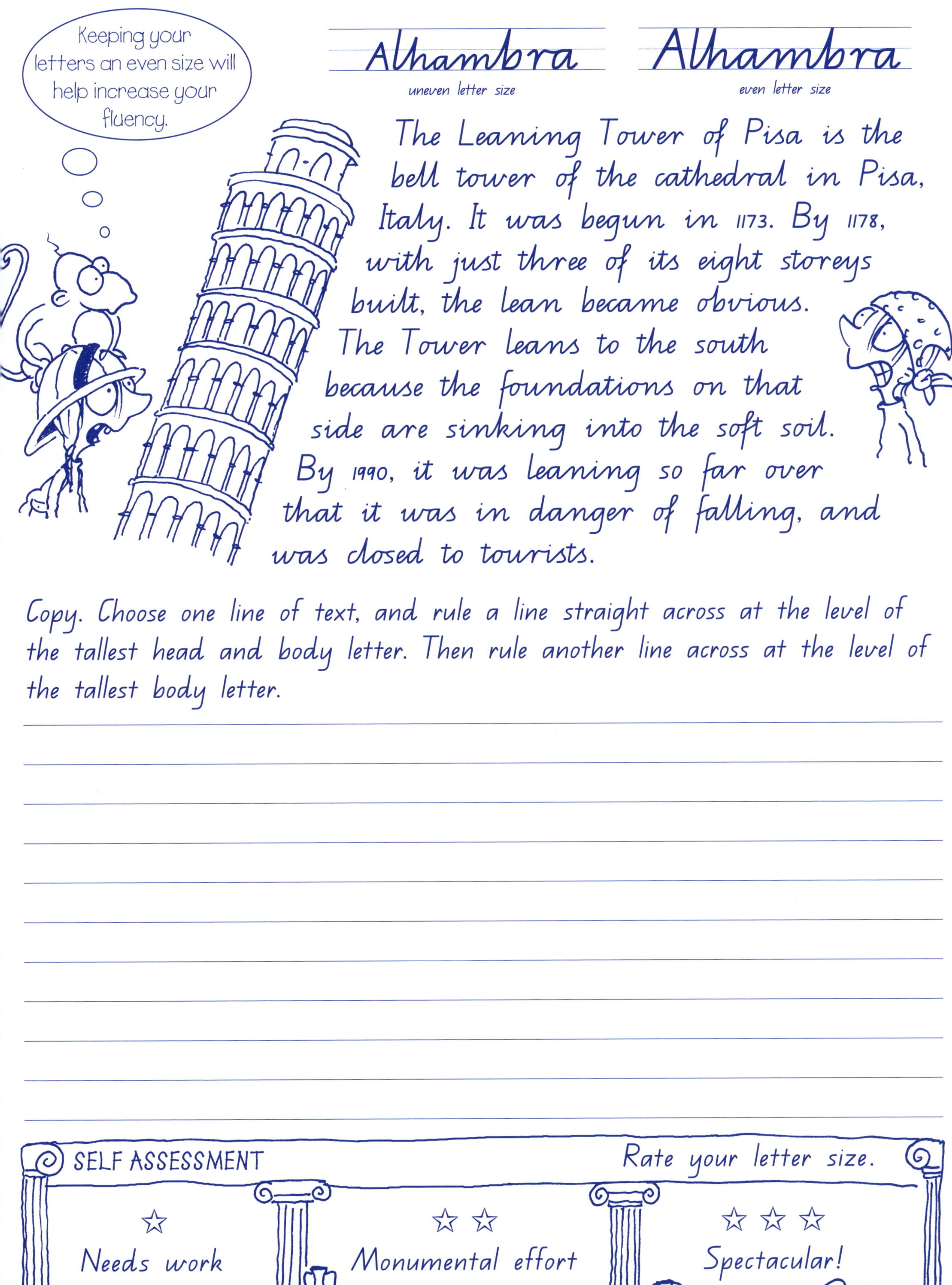

The Leaning Tower of Pisa is the bell tower of the cathedral in Pisa, Italy. It was begun in 1173. By 1178, with just three of its eight storeys built, the lean became obvious. The Tower leans to the south because the foundations on that side are sinking into the soft soil. By 1990, it was leaning so far over that it was in danger of falling, and was closed to tourists.

Copy. Choose one line of text, and rule a line straight across at the level of the tallest head and body letter. Then rule another line across at the level of the tallest body letter.

SELF ASSESSMENT

Rate your letter size.

☆	☆☆	☆☆☆
Needs work	Monumental effort	Spectacular!

Date ___ / ___ / ___

In 1999, engineers made another attempt to fix the Leaning

Tower of Pisa. This time they carefully took soil out from

under the north side of the Tower. It worked! The Tower

is now a bit straighter and more stable, and should be

safe for at least 200 years.

SELF ASSESSMENT

Tick the line with the best letter spacing.

Date ___ /___ /___

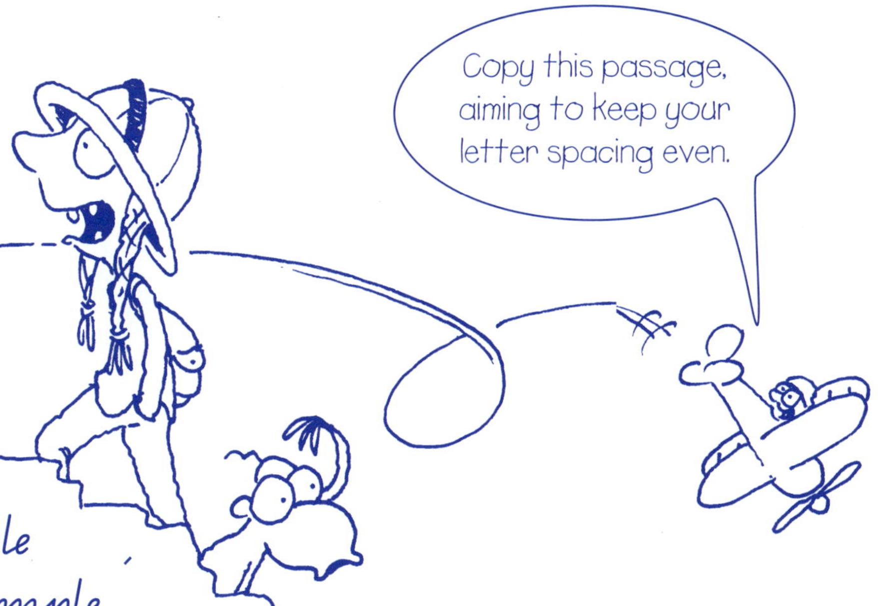

Copy this passage, aiming to keep your letter spacing even.

The Ancient Egyptians weren't the only ones to build pyramids. The Aztecs also built them – the Great Temple of Tenochtitlan, for example. Although only a fifth as tall as the Great Pyramid of Giza, this amazing structure was still an impressive size, being 30 metres high. One of the two temples at the top was dedicated to Huitzilopochtli, the god of the Sun and of war.

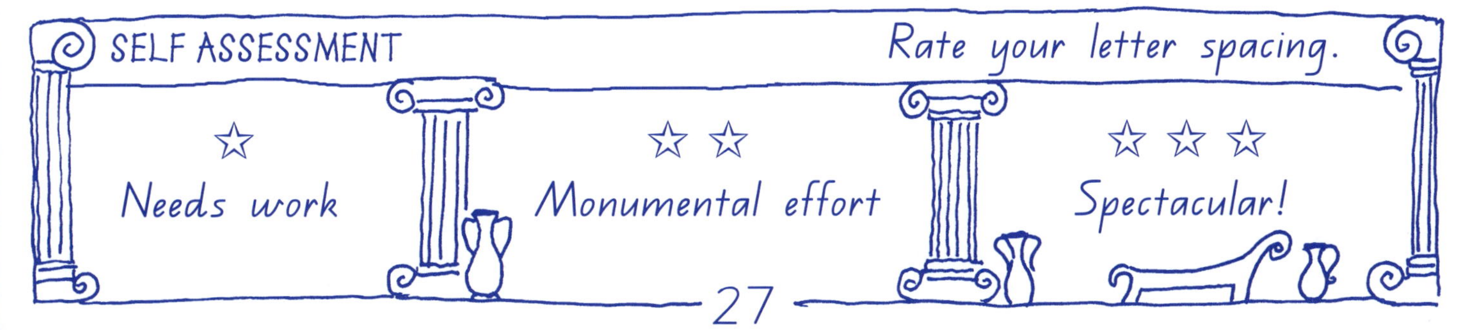

Date ___ / ___ / ___

The o ten o chapels o have o colourful o domes. ← good spacing

The ten chapels have colourful domes. ← o's won't fit between words

The o ten o chapels o have o colourful o domes. ← too spacy

St Basil's Cathedral in Moscow was built in the 1550's on

the orders of Tsar Ivan IV, also known as "Ivan the

Terrible". It contains chapels topped with colourful,

patterned domes. The onion shape of the domes stops the

roofs collapsing under heavy snow.

SELF ASSESSMENT

Use a highlighter pen to highlight the line with the best word spacing.

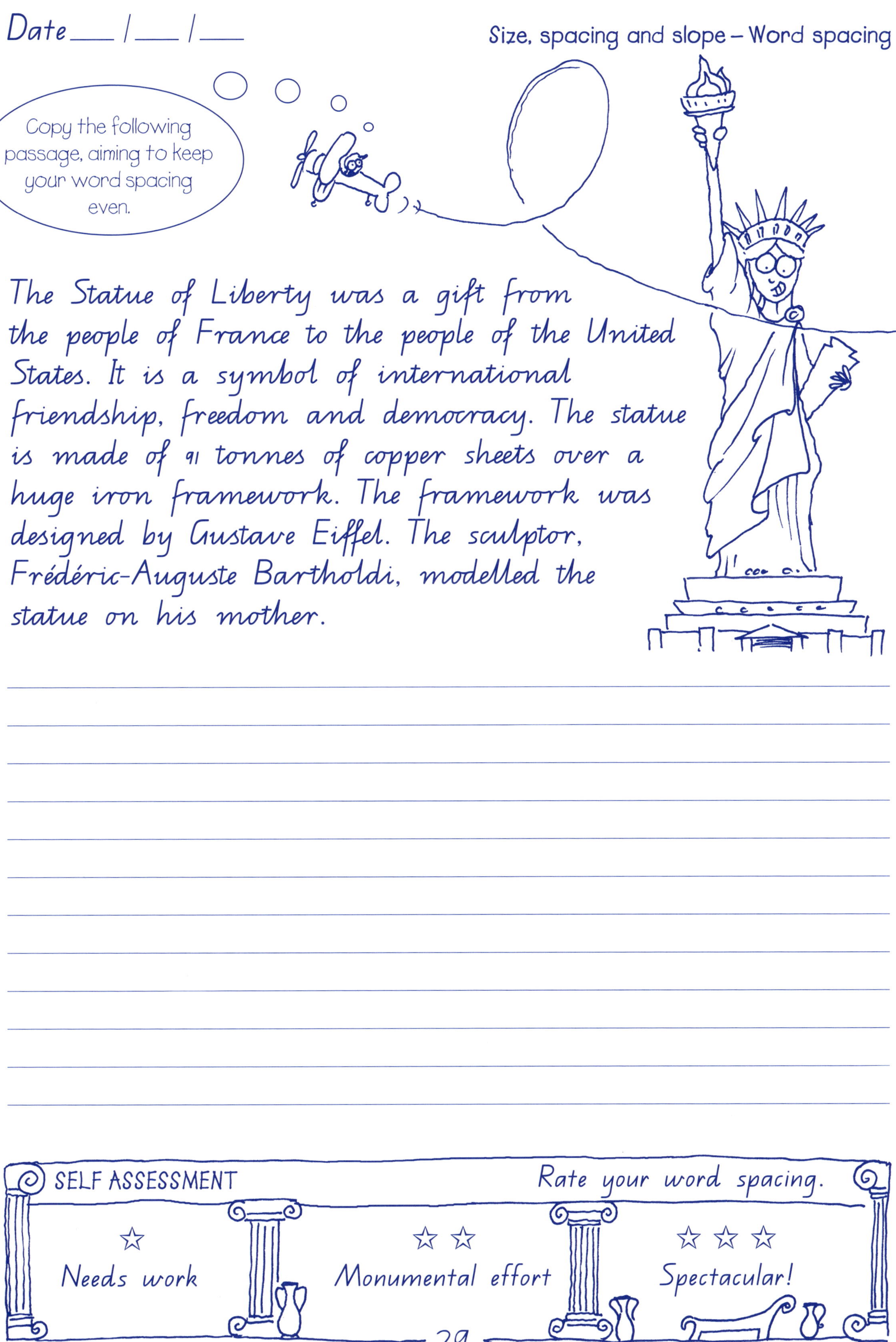

The Statue of Liberty was a gift from the people of France to the people of the United States. It is a symbol of international friendship, freedom and democracy. The statue is made of 91 tonnes of copper sheets over a huge iron framework. The framework was designed by Gustave Eiffel. The sculptor, Frédéric-Auguste Bartholdi, modelled the statue on his mother.

SELF ASSESSMENT

Rate your word spacing.

☆ Needs work

☆☆ Monumental effort

☆☆☆ Spectacular!

Date ___ / ___ / ___

Keeping the slope of your writing consistent makes it a lot easier to read.

Look at the words below. Circle the words that have a consistent slope.

blazing party sandwich break peach skin parcel

slippery pudding bumps soapy babble deepest spring

Copy the passage below. Remember to keep your slope consistent.

The Galápagos Islands are found in the eastern Pacific

Ocean. They are famous for their beauty, and for the

variety and uniqueness of the plants and animals there.

Some species are only ever found on specific islands in

this group.

Rate your letter and word spacing.

☆ ☆☆ ☆☆☆

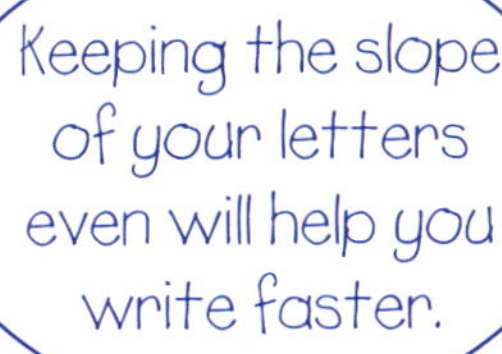

When you have copied the text, choose one line and check your slope by ruling lines along the downstrokes of the letters.

The Taj Mahal stands in Agra, India. Emperor Shah Jahan had it built in memory of his favourite wife, Mumtaz Mahal. It now contains both their bodies. The Taj Mahal is built entirely of white marble. It is said to be indescribably beautiful, especially at dawn and at sunset.

Date ___ / ___ / ___

Write this passage out in cursive. Then:

- ☆ choose one line and add a dot at each point where your writing touches the baseline
- ☆ choose another line and write an o between each word
- ☆ choose another line and rule lines along the downstrokes.

Keli Mutu lies on the island of Flores in Indonesia. The volcano at Keli Mutu is still active, and three lakes fill its three craters. The amazing thing about them is that each lake is a different colour. One of the lakes was originally a rich glowing red, but has got gradually darker and is now almost black. The lake next to it is an opaque emerald green. The third lake is a transparent sparkling green.

Teacher

Date ___ / ___ / ___

Speed test 

Look at the sentence and memorise it if you can. Copy it as many times as you can in 2 minutes. Have a classmate time you.

The Alhambra in Spain is a beautiful palace that includes a fortress, courtyards, gardens and fountains.

Total number of words: ________

Divide by two for speed in words per minute: ________

Rate your fluency.

☆ ☆☆ ☆☆☆

Rate your legibility.

☆ ☆☆ ☆☆☆

 Date ___ / ___ / ___

Pencil lifts, like at drop-on joins or after capital letters, give your hand a break. They also give you a chance to move your hand across the page.

Move your hand and arm across together – don't bend your hand back at the wrist.

Choose one line and make a mark like this ʹ above each place you will lift your pencil. Then copy.

Before the Panama Canal was built, ships had to sail right around the bottom of South America to travel between the Atlantic and Pacific Oceans. The 82km Canal can cut travelling distances by up to 12,875km! It cut sailing times from roughly six months to six weeks.

SELF ASSESSMENT

Do your hand and arm move across together?

Yes No Sometimes

Diagonal joins are the most common kind of join. To make your writing faster and smoother, make your diagonal joins go to the next letter at a 45 degree angle.

Stone circles such as Stonehenge may have been burial places, as well as places used for astronomical calculations. One of the weirder wonders of the world is Carhenge, in Nebraska, U.S.. It's a copy of Stonehenge made from old cars. Jim Reinders, a farmer and artist, built Carhenge as a memorial to his dead father.

SELF ASSESSMENT

Rate your diagonal joins.

☆ ☆☆ ☆☆☆

Rate your fluency.

☆ ☆☆ ☆☆☆

Date ___ / ___ / ___

One day in 1938, a fisherman near Madagascar caught a strange fish. A visiting scientist spotted the fish, which was found to be a coelacanth. These large fish have heavy, dull blue scales and lobed fins – and were thought to have been extinct for 70 million years! Finding one was like "finding a live dinosaur roaming the earth".

Date___ /___ /___

Your writing will be more legible if the horizontal joins from o, r, v and w have just a small dip.

The Grand Canyon in Arizona, U.S., is one of the most spectacular of the world's natural wonders. It's unbelievably enormous — 1.6km deep and 15km wide. It has taken millions of years for the Colorado River to gouge out this huge channel. In the process, many layers of rock have been exposed. The layers are in striking colours, and these colours change with the light and the season.

SELF ASSESSMENT

Rate your horizontal joins.

☆ ☆☆ ☆☆☆

Rate your word spacing.

☆ ☆☆ ☆☆☆

Date ___ / ___ / ___

Remember to retrace the top of the s after a horizontal join, and to use the modified s after a diagonal join.

Kakadu National Park is a vast wilderness. Much of the land belongs to the Gagudju people, who have lived there for over 40,000 years. Kakadu's landscape features cliffs, ravines and waterfalls, as well as grasslands, forests, swamps and rivers. If you visit, beware of the saltwater crocodiles – they'll attack anything that comes too close!

Date___ /___ /___

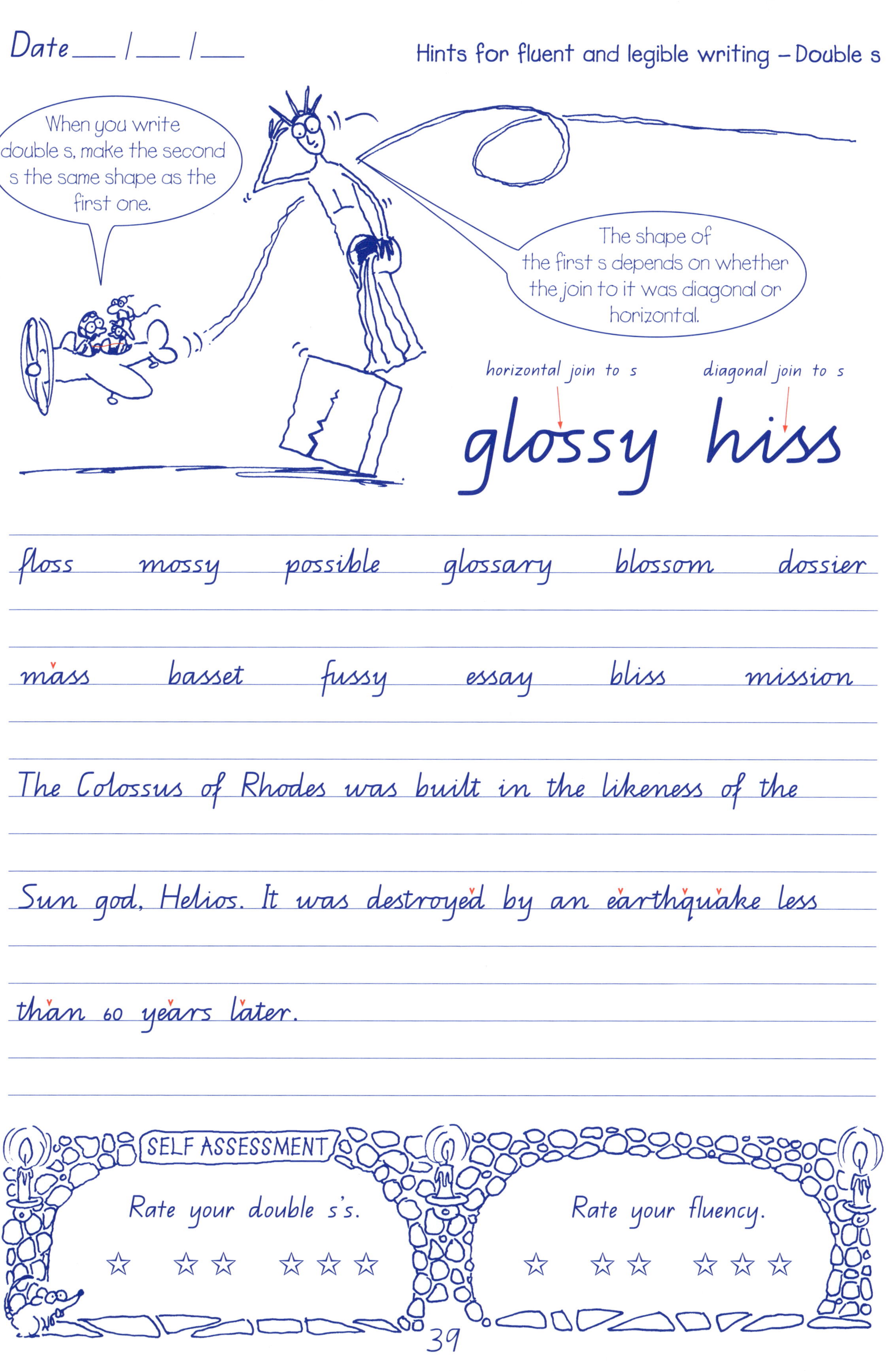

floss mossy possible glossary blossom dossier

mass basset fussy essay bliss mission

The Colossus of Rhodes was built in the likeness of the Sun god, Helios. It was destroyed by an earthquake less than 60 years later.

SELF ASSESSMENT

Rate your double s's.

☆ ☆☆ ☆☆☆

Rate your fluency.

☆ ☆☆ ☆☆☆

Date ___ / ___ / ___

When you write double f, you can go on to join from the second crossbar as you would from the crossbar of a single f.

join from crossbar

Another rather different wonder is the world's largest collection of navel fluff. Since 1984, Australia's Graham Barker has managed to collect 15.41 g of his own navel fluff. While some may scoff, or find collecting navel fluff a daft hobby, for Graham it's just part of his daily routine. Graham's goal is to gather enough of the soft fluff to stuff a cushion.

SELF ASSESSMENT

Circle your best joined double f.
Tick the line that has the most consistent slope.

small dip

rr

The letter r has a rounded entry. When r joins to another r, a small dip occurs.

arr barrier arr carry arr quarry

err territory err error err interrupt

irr irrational irr mirror orr correct

orr corridor orr tomorrow urr scurry

Many tourists visit the Northern Territory to marvel at its terrific geological features. This impressive terrain includes amazing landforms like Uluru and Kata Tjuta.

SELF ASSESSMENT

Rate your double r's.

☆ ☆☆ ☆☆☆

Rate your fluency.

☆ ☆☆ ☆☆☆

Date ___ / ___ / ___

ee needle ee weekly ee succeed

ee screen ee teenager ee Queensland

ee weekend ee oversee ee seeking

When writing double o, remember to retrace the top of the second o.

oo foolish oo shampoo oo cartoon

oo mushroom oo footprint oo oozes

oo boomerang oo football oo cooking

SELF ASSESSMENT

Circle your best double e and double o.

Don't cramp up the join from m to m. Keep the letters evenly spaced.

mm ✓ mm ✗

mm summit mm commute mm symmetry

mm plummet mm immigrate mm shimmer

mm community mm ammonia mm flammable

When you write double n, keep your slope consistent.

inn ✓ inn ✗

nn annual nn banner nn announcer

nn punnet nn channel nn skinny

nn cannon nn innings nn penny

SELF ASSESSMENT

Rate your double m's.

☆ ☆☆ ☆☆☆

Rate your double n's.

☆ ☆☆ ☆☆☆

Hints for fluent and legible writing – Double l, double t

Date ___ / ___ / ___

fill — even slope

attack — come back and do the crossbar last

Keep the slope of the letters even, and remember to cross double t with one crossbar.

all ell ill oll ull all ell ill oll

traveller illustrate college bellow gully swallow

att ett itt ott utt att ett itt ott

rattle settlement glitter pottery gutter attack

The Matterhorn is a spectacular mountain on the Italian-Swiss border. Herman Perren, a fellow from nearby Zermatt, attempted to tally 150 climbs. He died on a climb less than 10 climbs short of his goal.

SELF ASSESSMENT

Rate your double l's.

☆ ☆☆ ☆☆☆

Rate your double t's.

☆ ☆☆ ☆☆☆

Date ___ / ___ / ___

To increase your fluency, dot your i's after you complete the word.

size — come back and dot the i last

sift swing skittle obtain cipher risky

aisle asteroid rubbish built nifty bliss

fitness twice thing timber while slipper

public chain practice circle limit finite

Not all of the amazing wonders of the world are discovered on land. Deep sea trenches contain fantastic landforms and animals.

SELF ASSESSMENT

Rate your legibility.

☆ ☆☆ ☆☆☆

Rate your fluency.

☆ ☆☆ ☆☆☆

Date ___ / ___ / ___

Where would you find thousands of limestone pillars standing in a desert? The answer is: in Western Australia! The Pinnacles are an extraordinary sight – every one is different. Some are the size of cars, and others are the size of your little finger. They are also all kinds of shapes, and some have been given names like "Camel", "Kangaroo", and "Molars".

SELF ASSESSMENT

Rate your punctuation.

☆ ☆☆ ☆☆☆

Rate your legibility.

☆ ☆☆ ☆☆☆

Date ___ / ___ / ___

When you're taking notes, you don't want your writing to be fancy – just fast! But you need it to be legible, so that when you go back you can read what you wrote.

Write this sentence out as many times as you can in a minute. Have a classmate time you.

Australia contains some of the most breathtaking natural wonders in the world.

Number of words ______ Legibility ☆ ☆☆ ☆☆☆

Sloping your writing a little bit more, while still keeping the slope even, can help you write faster. So can spacing your words out a bit more.

Copy the sentence again as many times as you can in a minute. This time slope your writing a little more, and leave a little more space between words.

Number of words ______ Legibility ☆ ☆☆ ☆☆☆

Date ___ / ___ / ___

Some common abbreviations:

& = and

+ = and

C^{21st} = 21st century

etc. = et cetera (This means "and other things".)

$\bar{w}$ = with

List some words you think it might be useful to abbreviate. Try out some abbreviations for them.

Which abbreviations would you like to experiment with some more?

Date ___ / ___ / ___

Write each word in cursive.

Diagonal joins

this minute splinter element flint tuner

Drop-on joins

dainty edges action sequel fades igloos

Horizontal joins

don't valley ruins woven roses detours

Double s and double f

amiss grass floss bossy gruff sniffed

Double r, double e and double o

barren carrot seen flee spoon scooter

Double n, double m and double t

tinned manners summit grammar little lottery

Write this sentence out as many times as you can in one minute. Remember to slope your writing a little more, and leave a little more space between words.

I would love to explore the wonders of the world.

Teacher

Date ___ / ___ / ___

Read the sentence below, and memorise it if you can. Write out the sentence as many times as you can in 2 minutes. Have a classmate time you.

> *A platypus is a natural wonder – a cat-sized egg-laying mammal with fur like a beaver, a duck's bill and webbed feet!*

Number of words: ________

Divide by two for speed in words per minute: ________

SELF ASSESSMENT

Rate your fluency.

☆ ☆☆ ☆☆☆

Rate your legibility.

☆ ☆☆ ☆☆☆

You can repeat this test on another sheet at a later date to see if your speed's increased. Remember to assess your legibility as well. Speed means nothing if you can't read the writing!

Flourished capitals are used in text you want to look fancy – not when you need to write quickly.

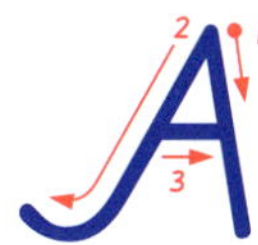 A A A A A

B B B B B B

 C C C C C

D D D D D D

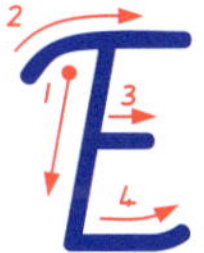 E E E E E

F F F F F F

 G G G G G

H H H H H H

 I I I I I

J J J J J J

 K K K K K

L L L L L L

M M M M M M

N N N N N N

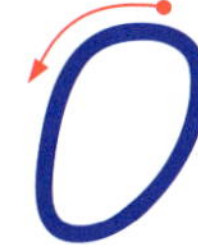 O O O O O

P P P P P P

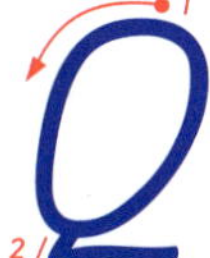 Q Q Q Q Q

R R R R R R

Date ___ / ___ / ___

S S S S S S

T T T T T T

U U U U U U

V V V V V V

W W W W W W

X X X X X X

Y Y Y Y Y Y

Z Z Z Z Z Z

Now practise writing flourished capitals.

A B C D E F G H I J K L M

N O P Q R S T U V W X Y Z

Write your name and address using flourished capitals for the capital letters.

SELF ASSESSMENT

Circle your best example of each flourished capital.

Date ___ / ___ / ___

You can add a decorative touch to the presentation of your writing by adding decorative strokes to your letters.

Copy these flourished letters.

b b b b b b b b b b b

d d d d d d d d d d d

f f f f f f f f f f f

h h h h h h h h h h h

k k k k k k k k k k k

l l l l l l l l l l l

p p p p p p p p p p p

SELF ASSESSMENT

Circle your best example of each flourished letter.

Date ___ / ___ / ___

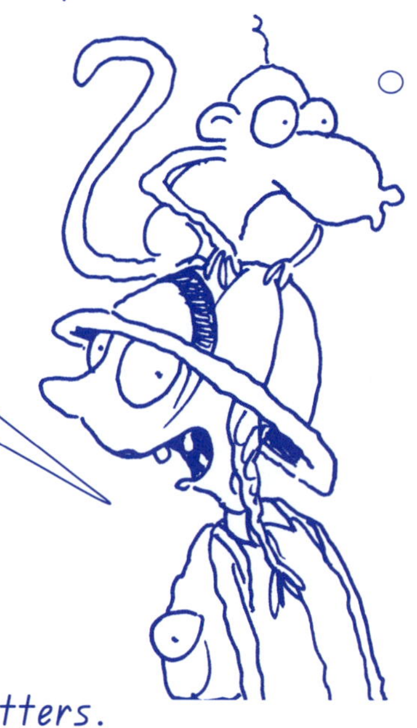

Practise these flourished letters.

b d f h k l p b d f h k l p

Now practise the flourished alphabet.

Aa Bb Cc Dd Ee Ff Gg Hh Ii

Jj Kk Ll Mm Nn Oo Pp Qq Rr

Ss Tt Uu Vv Ww Xx Yy Zz

Write the names of some people you admire, using flourished letters.

SELF ASSESSMENT

Rate your flourished writing.

☆ ☆☆ ☆☆☆

Want to explore this technique further?

Yes No Maybe

Date ___ / ___ / ___

Label this diagram of the south route to the summit of Mt Everest.

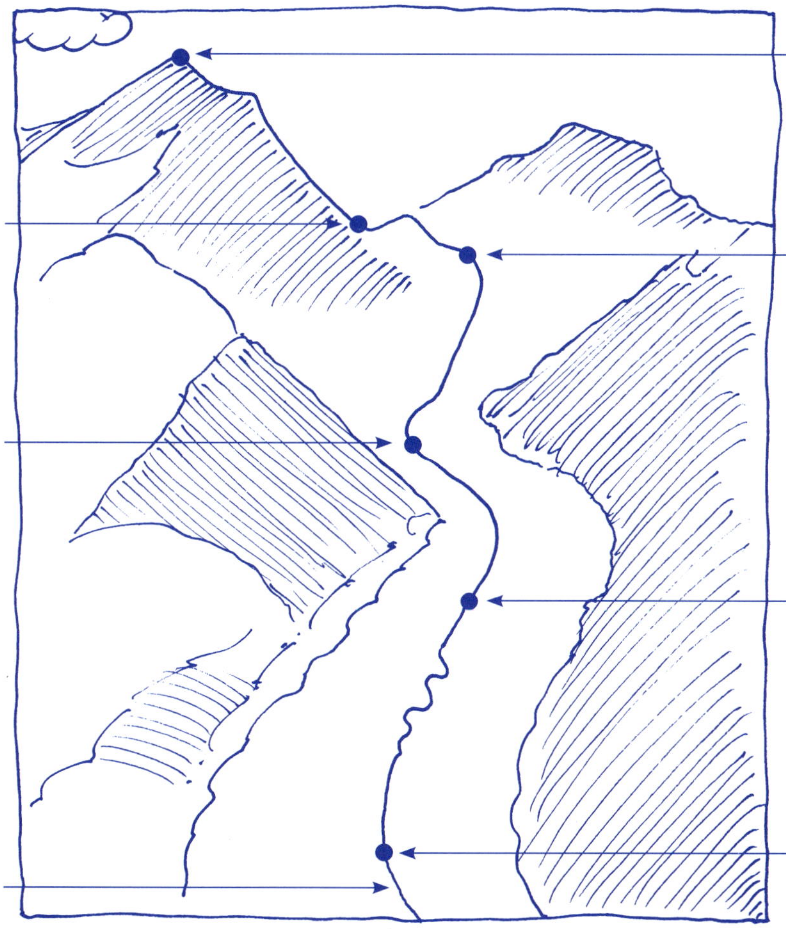

Base Camp (5,395m) Camp I (6,066m) Camp II (6,492m)
Camp III (7,468m) Camp IV (7,925m) Summit (8,850m)
Route to the summit

Date ___ / ___ / ___

Label this diagram of a mountaineer's equipment, using printing script. Then write out the list of equipment in cursive.

clothing in layers	lightweight, flexible boots	
gaiters	waterproof backpack	sun protection
sleeping mat	water bottle	helmet

Equipment list

Date ___ /___ /___

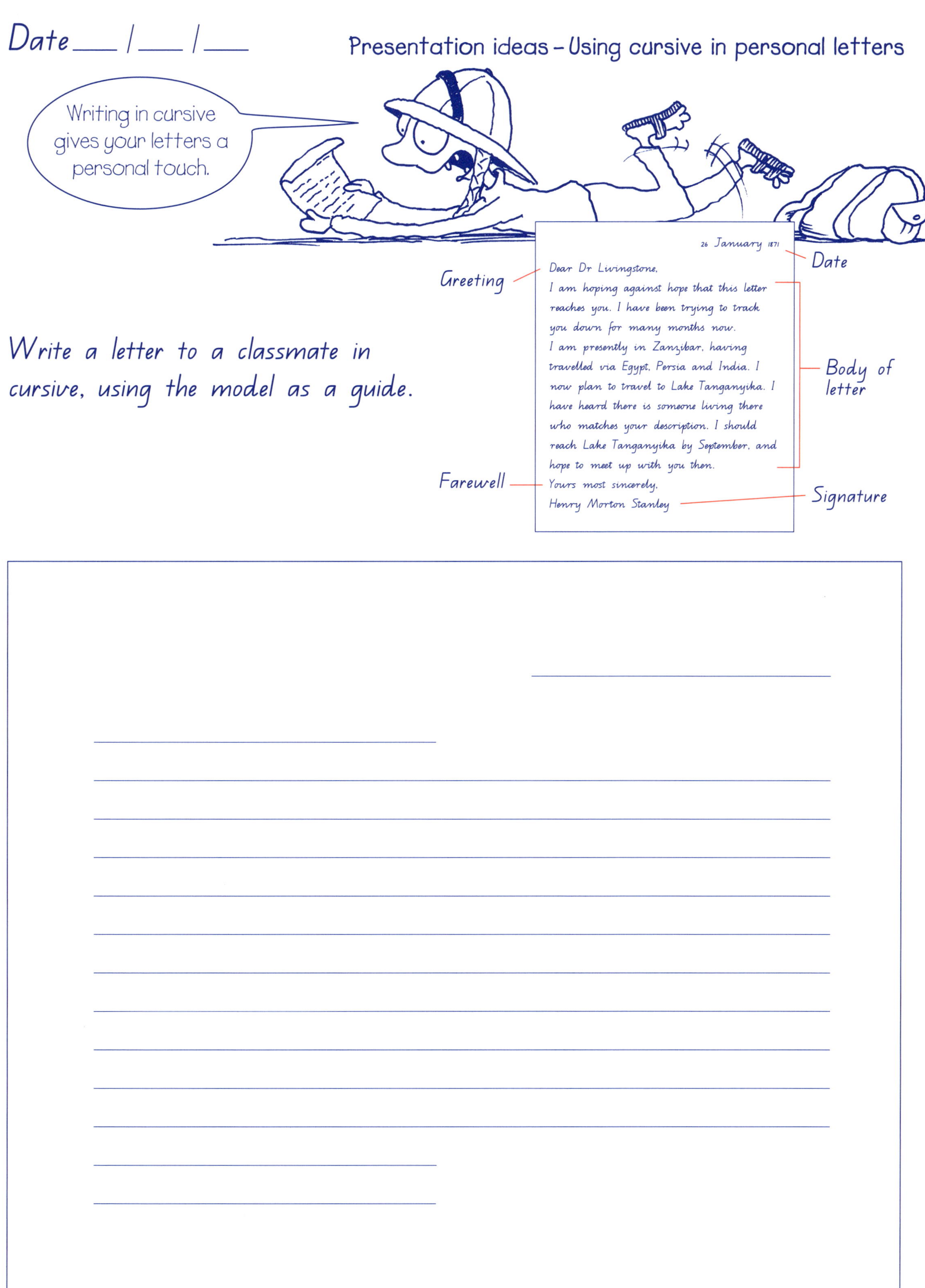

Write a letter to a classmate in cursive, using the model as a guide.

Presentation ideas – Using different writing instruments

Date ___ / ___ / ___

Select 5 different writing instruments from the box below.

> * metal nib pen * ballpoint pen * felt-tip pen * H pencil * HB pencil * 2B pencil * 3B pencil * short pencil * long pencil * thick-barrelled pencil * coloured pencil

Complete the table below by copying the sentence using the 5 different writing instruments.

Writing instrument	Writing instruments influence my writing.

★ Place a tick ✓ beside the writing instrument that you found easiest to use and that produced your neatest work.

★ Place a cross ✗ beside the writing instrument that you found hardest to use and that produced the messiest work.

Grand Canyon National Park Internal Aviation
FLIGHT REQUEST FORM

NAME: ____

ADDRESS: ____

____

PILOT LICENCE NO.: ______________________________

DAY, DATE AND TIME FLIGHT IS REQUESTED: __________

____

PASSENGERS' NAMES: ______________________________

1. ____
2. ____
3. ____

CARGO ITEMS AND WEIGHTS:

1. ______________________________ / ______ kg
2. ______________________________ / ______ kg
3. ______________________________ / ______ kg
4. ______________________________ / ______ kg

REASON FOR FLIGHT: ______________________________

____

SIGNATURE: ____________________ DATE: __________

NOTE TO TRIP ORGANISER: IF FLIGHT IS APPROVED, THE COMPLETED AND SIGNED FORM MUST BE AT THE HELIBASE BY FLIGHT TIME.

Date ___ / ___ / ___

UNDERGROUND

Choose four of the titles below, and create a different style of heading for each.

The Curse of the Mummy's Tomb
Leaning Tower Finally Topples!
How to Spot a Coelacanth
Thoughts of a Navel Fluff Collector
Why the Dead Sea is So Salty
Come to Stunning Keli Mutu!

One way to design a border is to design an element that is then repeated right around the border.

Don't make the element too fancy, or the border will take forever to do! And simple borders are often the most effective.

This is the element that has been repeated to create the border around this page.

Design two border elements, then see how they each look in an extended section.

Date ___ / ___ / ___

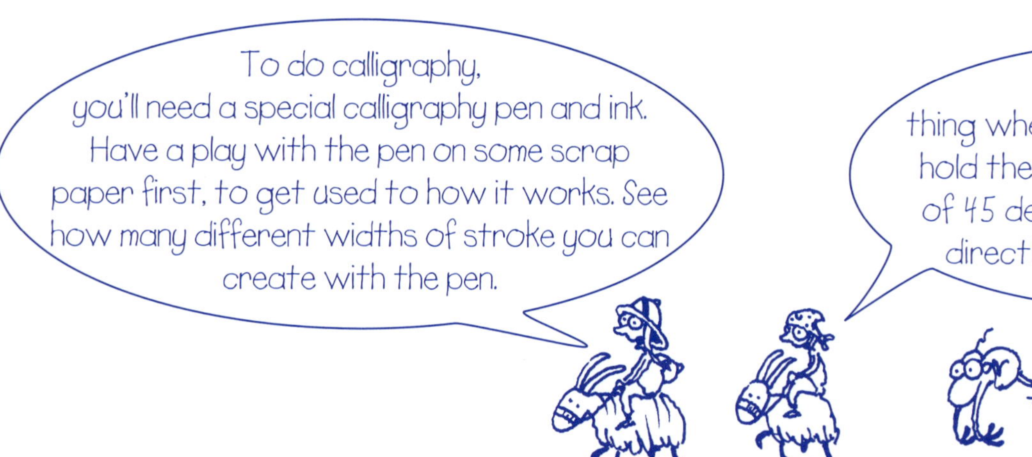

Try out these strokes, remembering to keep your pen at an angle of 45 degrees.

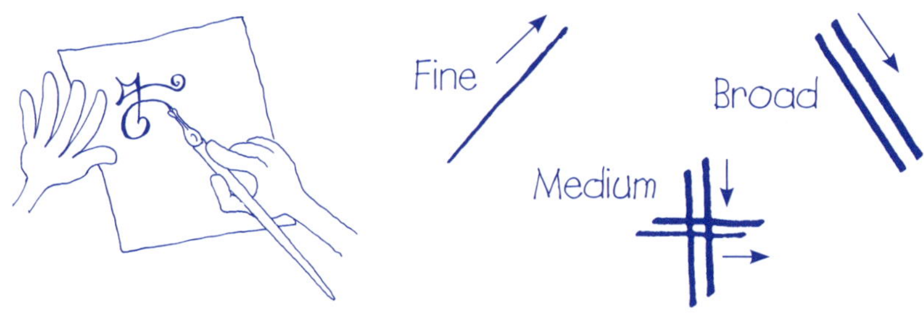

Try copying these letters. The capitals are called uncials, and the lower-case version are half uncials.

A B C D E F G H I J K L M

N O P Q R S T U V W X Y Z

a b c d e f g h i j k l m

n o p q r s t u v w x y z

Date ___ /___ /___

Use your calligraphy pen and uncial script to address this envelope to a friend, and write your own name and address on the back.

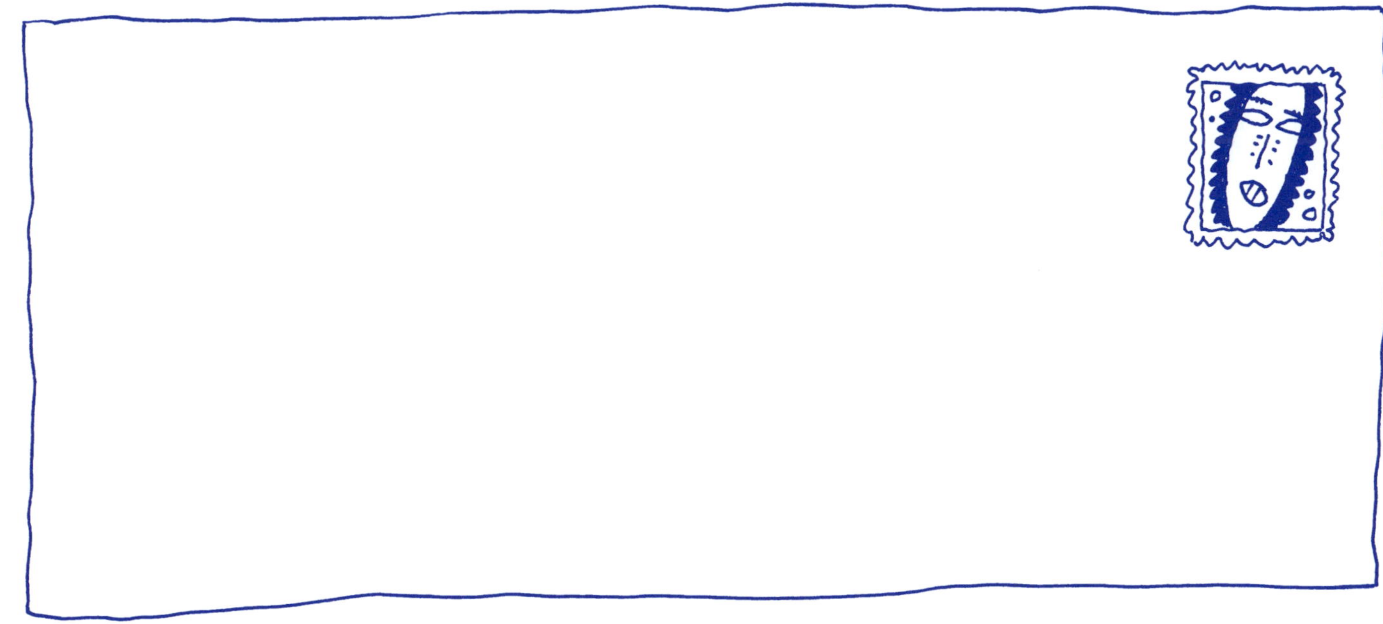

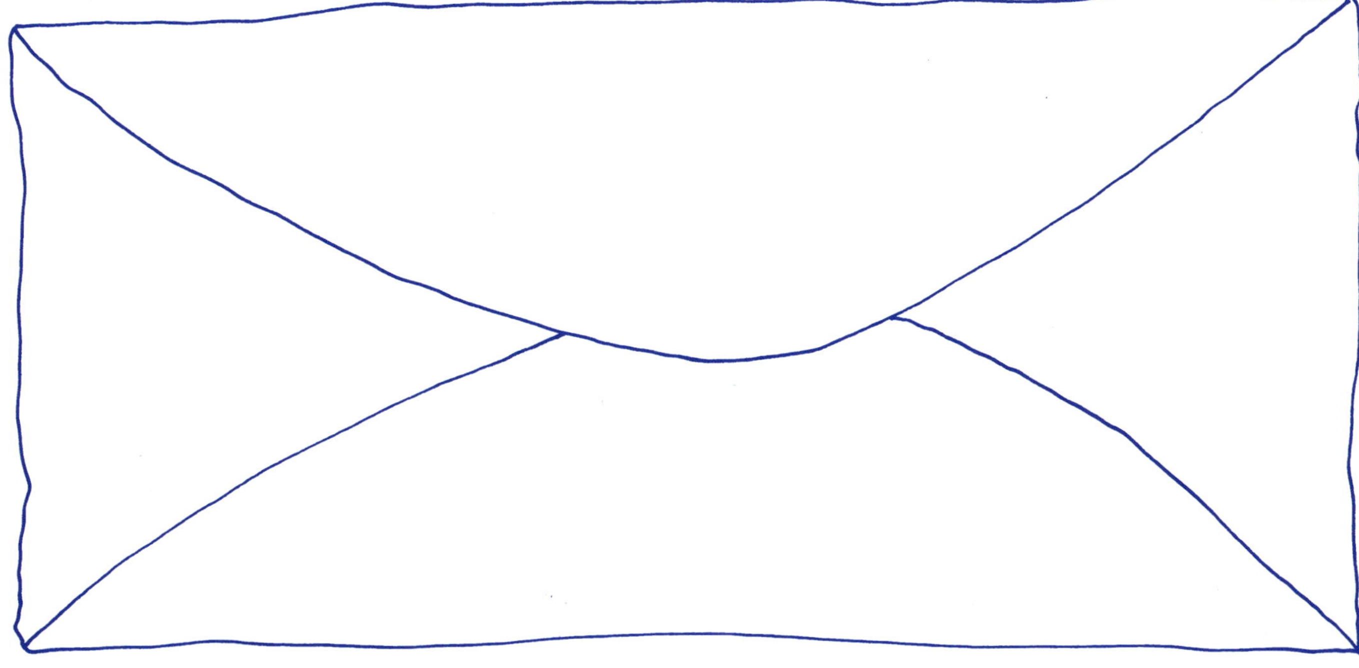

Date ___ /___ /___

At the end of the year, collect autographs from the people in your class. An autograph can simply be a signature, or can include a funny message or rhyme.

Autographs